A Den Is a Bed for a Bear

A Book About Hibernation

BY

BECKY **BAINES**

 NATIONAL GEOGRAPHIC

A den can be
a nest in a cave,

Some bears bring leaves
and grass into their dens to make
them nice and comfy.

There are lots of
different kinds of bears.

Grizzly bears
are a kind of
brown bear.

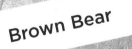
Brown Bear

in the snow,

Polar Bear

female
polar bear

Only female polar bears
use dens, and only if they
are ready to have cubs.

6

Black Bear

or under a tree!

7

A den is a bed
that a bear will build

(where no one else will be).

KEEP OUT!

You don't want
to bother a
sleepy bear!

A den is a place
a bear will go

A polar bear's favorite
meal is seal!

Black bears usually eat
plants, berries, or bugs.

...when they eat until their bellies are **full**

(because soon there'll be no food at all).

WINTER AHEAD EAT UP!

During the fall, bears may eat up to 20,000 calories a day. That's like eating 65 cheeseburgers in one day!

A den is a place to hibernate:

Z z z Z Z

14

to sleep the winter through.

Other bears don't hibernate because where they live there is plenty of food all year long.

It's a place a bear
can be snug
and warm and have
her babies, too.

Mother bears have their cubs in the den,
and sometimes don't even wake up.

Most cubs are twins, although bears
can also have three or four cubs.

actual size

When cubs are born, they weigh less than a pound.

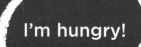

I'm hungry!

Too helpless
for winter ahead,
but cozy and fed in
their bear of a bed.

Cubs are born with their
eyes shut, but they find the
way to their mother's milk.

As months go by,
the cubs grow strong and
much bigger every day.

When spring begins and mom wakes up,

they're ready to go out and play.

Mom is hungry. She hasn't eaten for months!

For **winter** is over and it's time for all **bears**

to leave their dark dens for the sun.

When they leave their den, cubs are about ten times bigger than when they were born.

In the **fresh** air, they can stretch their legs

TAG! You're it!

And eat!
And climb!
And run!

But an empty den
isn't empty for long.

When summer
  is over and fall's
in the air,

a new mama bear
    might make it her lair...

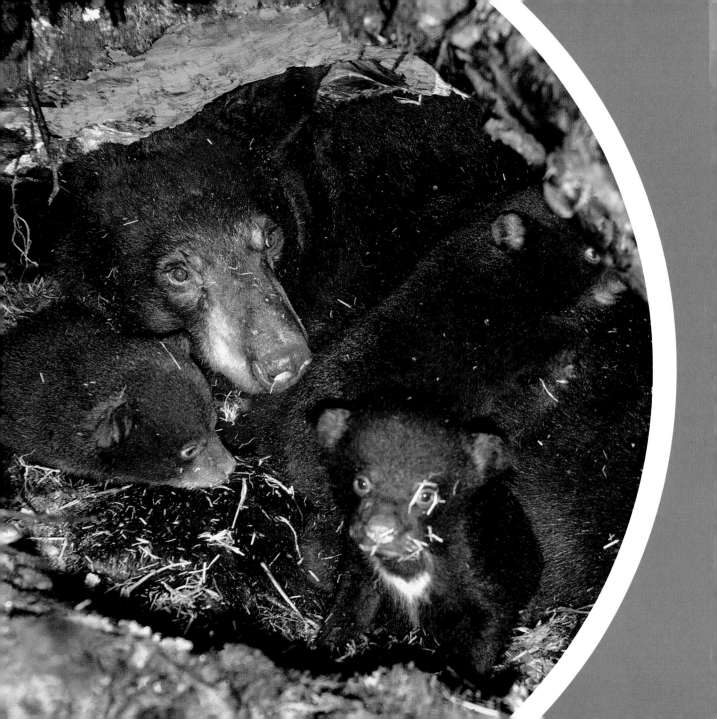

...because a den
is a bed for a bear!

Zigzag through these ideas for more thoughts about bears and hibernation.

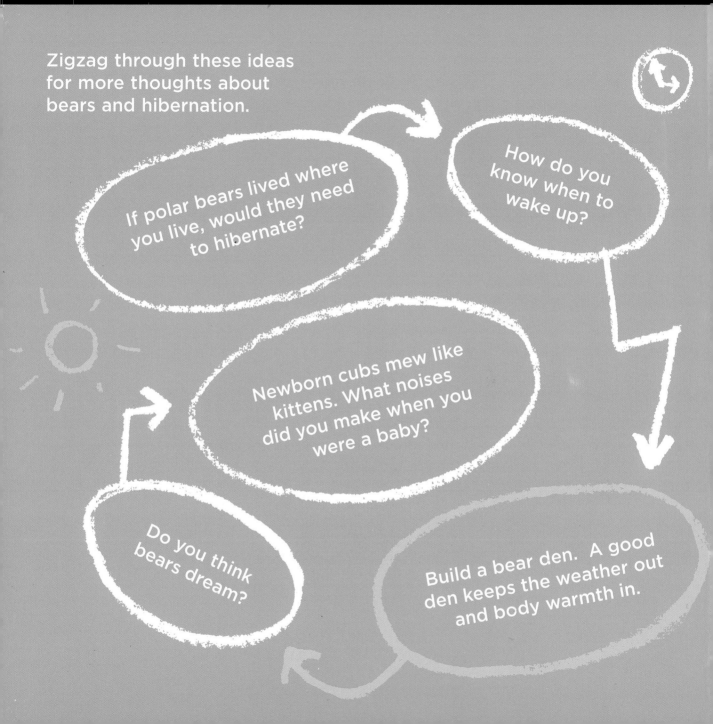

If polar bears lived where you live, would they need to hibernate?

How do you know when to wake up?

Newborn cubs mew like kittens. What noises did you make when you were a baby?

Do you think bears dream?

Build a bear den. A good den keeps the weather out and body warmth in.